"The first thing you notice about David Breskin is that he's got chops up the wazoo and is fabulously intelligent. It may take longer to start seeing through his fierce and faceted eye or to notice how many of our lived-in worlds it sees in all their dazzle of simultaneity and fact. This is poetry in which the intimate and public worlds do not exclude each other but mutually refract their signs and lights, and where even the self on which the world imposes its unrelenting politics can earn, with ingenuity and effort, its meed of radiance."

—Rafi Zabor, author of *The Bear Comes Home*,
PEN/Faulkner Award Winner

"In David Breskin's *Escape Velocity*, ferocity and speed don't preclude clarity of critique, and the tectonic instabilities of metaphor's capacity for disruption is married to a clarity of focus, producing a vivid, Baroque pageantry that defies chronology in favor of synchronicity, that gives us panoramas of wrecks. Rare to find poetry that is so confrontational, so avid to go to the hot spots, to risk being brutal in the service of truth while preserving such formal elegance. Unflinching, these poems roar like Cassandra with disastrous moment: it's a transfixing sound."

—Dean Young, author of *Skid*

"David Breskin's *Escape Velocity* is torqued with rage at the world as he finds it, 'a micro avalanche of each soul's presence.' With formal precison and clarity, he elucidates the sorrows of our times, an unflinching and brave indictment of the spoils of life's wars, both personal and political. Underneath the polemics is a poet's love: 'your future / your child, this infancy of your desire.'"

—Ann Lauterbach, MacArthur Fellow and
author of *If in Time: Selected Poems 1975–2000*

ESCAPE VELOCITY

ESCAPE VELOCITY
David Breskin

Soft Skull Press
Brooklyn, NY | 2004

Published by Soft Skull Press | www.softskull.com
Distributed by Publishers Group West | www.pgw.com | 800.788.3123

Printed in Canada

Front cover image: "A Southern Chain Gang," 1903, photographer unknown,
Detroit Publishing Company Archives, Library of Congress #LC-D401-16155
Back cover image (detail): "Waiting for the Sunday Boat," 1902, William Henry
Jackson, Detroit Publishing Company Archives, Library of Congress #LC-D4-9116

Book Design: David Janik

Library of Congress Cataloging-in-Publication Data
Breskin, David.
 Escape velocity / by David Breskin.
    p. cm.
  ISBN 1-932360-45-X (trade cloth : alk. paper) -- ISBN 1-932360-44-1 (trade
pbk. : alk. paper)
  I. Title.
PS3552.R3878E83 2004
811'.54--dc22
                                        2004013825

ACKNOWLEDGMENTS

My thanks are given to the following publications, where these poems previously appeared, some in slightly different form:

ACM: "Newsworthy," "Hush-Harbor (The Old South)"

American Letters & Commentary: "Relevancy"

Bathos Review: "Ugly Beauty"

Boulevard: "Counting"

Columbia Poetry Review: "S, M, L, XL," "Diplomatic Relations"

CrossConnect: "My Prosthetic Everest"

Denver Quarterly: "Her, For Instance," "Revolutionary Politics"

Fourteen Hills: "Proclivity," "Invitation to Move West," "Rated X"

Harvard Review: "The Jug Shop"

The Minnesota Review: "Work," "Package / Packaging"

New American Writing: "State of Affairs of State," "The Architecture of Implosion," "Jumping Over Your Shadow Slash Landscape With Squeegee"

The Paris Review: "Broken Country Scramble"

Parnassus: Poetry in Review: "Capsized"

Poetry Flash: "Edge City," "Man, in the Middle of the Ocean, With Piano"

Press: "Pirates"

Quarterly West: "Failures," "Growing," "An Atmosphere of Isabel," "Belief Systems"

Southwest Review: "Double Blind"

Spelunker Flophouse: "Way Back in the Vanguard"

TriQuarterly: "Escape Velocity," "Literary Fiction," "Welfare Reform," "The Guitarist"

Thirty-four bars of praise for those whose buzzing feedback made these songs better: James McManus, W.S. Di Piero, Max Levchin, Isabel Breskin, Richard Eoin Nash, Nigel Poor.

CONTENTS

for Gerhard Richter

Prelude. . . . .

THE GUITARIST

for Bill Frisell

The guitarist goes home to the old home
where his father died. Gutbucket hospital

blues, loose change of cousins wandering
on the porch, call-and-response holler

of undertaker: this is the score of January
airplane, Carolina rain. Why some gigs

turn out the way they do is mystery
science theater of road, food and sleep. Why

certain notes attack other notes—certain
cells attack other cells—is not answered

in woodshed or studio, or on the phone
while mother gently weeps, but lies instead

against the grain of fret and neck unknown.
Slow amoeba of solo, with feedback,

against and inside the thrashing time
of drummer's snare and tom, ventures a guess.

Anaphora chorus, cilia of grace
notes swimming with echo: each song constructs

a better place, like silence above
shouting. The guitarist carries his axe

with him at all times, into the forest
of funeral, into the Douglas fir

and weeping willow, live oak, sycamore,
because in the end your chops are all

you have against the skirling tone-deaf world:
hammer, pluck, chord, gouge, pedal, ring, sustain.

JUMPING OVER YOUR SHADOW SLASH LANDSCAPE WITH SQUEEGEE

Knockdown-dragout tween arched guitar and fatback drums, a bass line
punches *the one* with thumbslap torque, wobbling excited atoms. Form
flows. Thanks for the straitjacket, always makes for a nice trip.
Awake on this phase-shifted ring-modulated morning, a plan
in hand from Control, we begin optimistically enough, on the off chance
weather will smile and our contrail write *PEACE* across azure. Who knows
whether our empennage will stresscrack or delam on climb out, sending eyes
scattering toward flames, waves, beryllium, faceless survivors, crushed hopes.

Ah, feathers of an arrow, shot high. An emperor penguin's hopes
lie on daddy's toes and momma, jammed with krill, making a swift return trip
from the leopard seal's bewhiskered rip-toothed scream-eyed
hunting ground: ice water. Talk about doubt! Mega-mega. Form
a circle, facing inward against sledgehammering wind. Only *ism* known
to work: mass cuddle. Like Mao, but less starvation no party line
sportier orange plumage. Getting a grip in sideways snow means chance
meetings, strangers in the night, the howling gist of a wedding plan.

Master say: *I could spend my life arranging things.* Spend, spend. Plan
A always comes with a lumpy dowry. Mascara rivulets puddling eyes
introduce Plan B to the shocked shocked participants. Hardly a chance
to catch breath after the stickymoon sojourn, a brochure-fringed trip
to empyrean isles (Darwin's wetspot dream) where each party's past toes the line
before rolling over in bed like a crushing blue-veined iceberg—the 10% hope
90% underwater surprise of every *James Caird* marriage. Riprap, swamp. The known
world can't compete. Then, at customs, upon re-entry, a most unusual form.

A scissoring. A sex change of robots. A restraining order. Form
follows fiasco. Brave men run in my family. Evers to Tinker to Chance.
Beserker manners: a careful riot, stockbrokers at a buffet whispering *Know
what? You gotta own it—GAARP, EBITDA.* But beauty's in the eye
of the bondholder. Suckers! He may have come from a place called Hope
but all night long it was honor, offer, honor, offer. The firebombing plan
for Dresden included Vonnegut and Richter as bit players, just boys, a story line
in the flick now showing at the Googolplex. A scissoring. A freaky trip.

Hanging round as Specktators, eight student nurses on an Illinois death trip.
Hanging against chambered walls, eight buckets of pulverized earth known
to the perp as dirty pictures. Exactly what—he axed anxiously—is your line
of work, sir? "Not *creating*, good god," having overheard the chance
remark about god being in the details. "More shattering windows: no health-plan
no normal hours though steady work where I grew up." But now conventions form
congealed sentiment: beat your *Kristall*rocks into shared squeegees, hope
you don't live to see the Reichstag's mirrored dome flaming your glass-flagged eye.

Luxe prison, hyperbaric cell, this prismatic retreat from the eye-for-an-eye
double-blind test of the dumb world's acne of failures. A fictive line
in the sand, real as razor wire. And how that floated line, with care, hopes
to relate to the next, and the next, and next next next, now known
to each other on courtly yet boppish terms, dancing through cruciformed
sphered starred fractals of light. Wrecktangles. Rhomboids. Squares. Trip-
wired triptychs springing traps on regiments of card-punching, retirement-plan
postmodernists. The skeptic's strange battle call? *Give paint a chance.*

Boogaloo. Shag. Frug. Swim. Lindy hop. Shimmy. Bump. Chance
encounters while dancing mix colors in ways only hoops and barbecue hope
to, blending egg and jizz in a get-down grisaille, the melting plan
we need for survival. See our possibilities? The best stem cell line
cooking in the fridge can't promise more than the miscegenation trip
overlayed twisty on a cold metal platter of deep South funk and high-eyed
Romantic North, every slab pulsing with wiggling zipping form,
slurred and slang color charts uncharted, remixed, not yet known.

Secede from the Either/Or. Join the Both/Ands, the Neither/Nors. What's known,
in the Biblical sense, accept, but shred the rest of that testament tomb. Plan
on a hard landing and the cynical gaze of those who cry "cynic." Form
no opinions that can't evolve like amphibians into upright facts. Hope
springs infernal, and occasionally those springs rust. That's when your *I*
needs all its crackbrained blowtorching spit to clean away craggy mischance—
lame barnacled hitchhiker relentlessly talking your ear off on every trip—
slip open the door and *push* . . . then pop some wheelies over the centerline.

Eye trip through your wires, skinned pupils, this functionless form
a snaking line round the block in a downpour of facts and beamed-eyes,
all just the planned chance of a steely, well-vetted chance plan.
Still, moving still: lookout for hope, alive in the superunknown.

GROWING

The static frizzle between sense and nonsense
is a sonic mulch much favored by fast-growing

meanings. Add rain and sun and next thing
you know, a riot of pansies and tenure. A swoop

to the hoop. Never rest on Everest. She was
the lighter, I was the cigarette. I was the spin

wave, she was the slumgullion. Upside down
decapitation: any Christmas tree cut

from earth to bear the cross of ornamental
sacrifice. And so on. To select certain

crystals amid the hard matrix of porphyry
speaks volumes. Volume one: personal prejudice.

Volume two: myopia and the corrective lens
of nurture. Volume three: an amp that goes

to eleven. Shiba Inu or schipperke, the pure
bred with the impure pees to mark its present:

the muttish bark of the new. Now a wandering
found when lost, now a deep blue florescence.

. . . . . . I . . . Evidence . . . .

ESCAPE VELOCITY

Thrust then blur, ripe speed, a gentle pricking
of atmosphere into the black yonder:

carrying a payload of past-due bills
from father, mother's invoice of regret,

the backyard family trash exploding up
out of a watery basement, where shelves sag

under the weight of time, you muscle past
aimless geese and grazing clouds, staking claim

to a future unpredicted by corner
commentators, those who'd have you flail

and fall. It could be ghetto. Could be bones
splintery since birth. Might be cross-eyed stairs

you couldn't climb, unsolved story problems,
the needle of hunger. Or just every

dull day flattening mind into a thin broth
of *No*. Whatever. To trigger ignition

in such conditions requires X. You are
Y. Go ahead and throttle Z round Z's

fat neck: smell the aggression of incline.
While your visored helmet rattles and fogs—

eyes hammered into sockets—a snaky
tether provides your vitals to the watching

few and the greater world awaiting. Life's
not cheap at this burn rate. Out here there's

no air save your own breath. You've gone so long
not talking, words feel like food in your mouth.

WELFARE REFORM

Mr. Full, I'm Mr. Empty. Rub my bones
together to spark a wispy fire. Swallow

your pride, keep yourself warm on the oil
of my intestine. Try a little garnish

of wages on the side. Not like North
Korea where they're so hungry women

eat their afterbirth. Not like Tutsi / Hutu
holocaust chutzpah. Here, just plaster

from project walls and Twinkies with food
stamps while trust fund babies quaff ecstasy

by the lake. Oh, those happy happy kids.
Mr. Empty on the cellphone, without two Franklins

to rub together, coming to you *live*. I'm
moving in. I'll be on your wraparound

mortgaged porch. I'll be walking little Ashley
to school, keeping her out of traffic

and trouble. I'll be your sleeping bag, your
makeup kit. The Lakota used every piece

of the buffalo and I expect no less
from you. If you rub me hard enough

against the rough concrete of the voters,
my skin comes off like grated cheese.

Recover the chaise. Patch the frayed cord
of the tennis net. Resole that old soft shoe.

UGLY BEAUTY

after Monk

Qwertyuiopasdfghjklzxcvbnm makes no sense yet
represents a certain kind of logic. Samewise

Dubya's tax-cut fervor, jowls of Dick jiggling
to its bulldozer bump and grind. Darwin

didn't go for hors d'oeuvres or cocktail party
pleasantries, but is an A-list guest these days

in better homes and gardens. His gyrations
at the Belle Curve Ball were quite a sight: lustrous

tux bursting at its seams so *down* was his white-
hot boogie fever. Still, quashing the calculators

of the skinny rich will not remove dead presidents
from their bank accounts. Exfoliating the mole

from Cindy Crawford's glowing puss will not keep girls
free of warts or safe from falling on icy slick

magazine covers. In her mingy pleasure den, Beauty
buffs the silver with her hot and bumptious breath.

NEWSWORTHY

The actress imploding in the strobed flash
of fame. Or the universe expanding, fat
with stars, showering down pinprick pulses

onto the Very Large Array, scattered
with sagebrush and defense dollars. Angle
of twist, angle of assault, in raking

light of print, flowers into breakfast
poppy, bright bulb'd coffee, a narcotic
of facts. The mean dance craze, untethered

astronauts, faulty Christmas lighting spark
jolly headlines bellying their gifts of good
and bad in measured doses. *If it bleeds, it leads.*

Cozy heartwrench of moms breast-feeding babies
crack, gap-toothed smiling toddlers falling
off roofs (shoved?), a high school winning streak

of gaudy soccer: come one, come all, mingle.
Turn the knife over morning's warm muffin
or shoes-off scotch. Bleed photos and fill dead

air. Freeze the market's dead-cat bounce and gush
fountains of guesswork on layoffs, key rates
of interest and disinterest, while surveying

space for the deeply personal, like poets
driving wives to suicide—*Extra! Extra!*
Not One, But Two!—in self-cleaning ovens.

DUE PROCESS

How much they owe you? Boy: fourteen, gawky,
braces, B+, shortstop, oboe, debate,

shot. Deep in the spleen of some insurance
office, there lies a chart. On it, numbers

sweating, making out with ravaged facts: math
of ravishment, revenge. Who can play and who

must pay are different answers to deflowered
questions. Here, sharp lawyers pause for truth

and lunch. Every third pickle, every third
slice of salami or fat wedge of king

salmon paid for. Every third bourbon, tank
of ultra, phone call, pen, power tie, ream

of glossy, briefcase or business-class seat:
the fruits of your meager tragedy. But who

can afford hourly fees or court costs?
Contingency's all. You've lost before

you've won. Only losing big makes winning
big possible. When the check finally knifes

into your account, years later, the tear
wakes mourning's slumber. You still can't drive by

that school. Each bell a pure defeat, a prick
of guilt and anger. You stay home, with time

money buys, and in your victory garden, grow
childless vacations: shame's plangent harvest.

MOSAIC WIPE (*Palm Beach Story*)

Like I said
Like I said sir
I just got these little bits and pieces
Little bits and pieces
Of memories

All I remember was getting through the gates

      Mosaic wipe
      Big blue dot

All I remember was being in the hiding spot
And seeing the little red light
All I remember is having a phone in my hand
And getting it to work

      Willie Horton
      Willie Smith

            Were you standing up or sitting down?
            Were you crouching down?
            Was it dark in the kitchen at the time?
            Did you have any difficulty dialing?

            Did he have any clothes on?
            Was he naked?
            When you said Will was trying to penetrate
            What position were your legs?

I don't know

Would you like a recess?

No

How did he manage to get your legs apart?
Would you like a recess?

No I would really like
To get this over with

When there is penetration
Was it difficult or easy?

It hurt me

Would you like a recess?

There's just a certain amount
Of emotional display
We're allowed to have
Step down and stretch
Step down and stretch for a bit for a moment

Was the ejaculation outside you or inside you?

Willie Horton
Willie Smith
William Kennedy Smith

Was that ejaculation inside your vagina
Or outside your vagina
Or both?

I don't know

Did you try as hard as you could
To prevent the act from occurring?

I tried as hard as I could

You were not sexually aroused?
Not lubricating?

No

Thank you

Mosaic wipe
Big blue dot
Seven-second delay

Was your strength any match
For his strength?
Were your legs any match
For his?

No no no no
I know I didn't have
My heels on in the house
Because I would have
Heard my heels clicking
On the linoleum

Billie sings *Hush now*
Don't explain
You're my joy and pain
Don't explain

Do you have any specific idea how
Those pantyhose came off?

JUST ASKING

If you could kill anyone and get away
with it, who would you kill? Would you choose to axe

an ex? Would dictators dictate your evening
plans? Buddhists in our audience may be horrified

but who are they to judge? Dung beetles, aardvarks,
pythons in past lives, now they slaughter plants

for supper, thinking nothing (of it). Protein
like me or Mussolini or a free-range

chicken can run away when threatened, but broccoli
doesn't stand a chance: chained to earth, blindfold

on, cigarette dangling, it nervously awaits
its firing squad of calloused immigrants. If you

can garrote squash or guillotine corn with a clean
conscience, then perhaps offing an executive

whose calloused eye for profits killed thousands
would not pose such a stretch. We only kill

what we eat, rifles back the hunter in the crowd,
thinking pheasant thoughts in full flight, not

revenge. But when you kill someone you consume
them, in a sense. The way they consumed you.

STATE OF AFFAIRS OF STATE (*The Blue Dress*)

Lamp black, flesh tint, scarlet lake, cobalt
violet: colors of the president's deep afternoon

nap dance under his elephant eyelids. Now thong
pink, rose madder, and coral orange betray

a deeper purpose far beneath his cerulean blue
window shades. When the Cabinet meets, sap

green runs from their mouths. When the Speaker
listens, raw umber coats his ears. A true

cadmium yellow provokes the jugular
press, while handlers run interference

red, interference blue, and titanium white
at network filters. Fugitive pigments

pledge allegiance to one view, then shift
in time's breeze to another, ruining harmony's

chorus of inclusion. The glass palette
of everyone's expectations shatters so jagged—

antique gold and iridescent silver spilling
to the floor—that the chief executive can

no longer patch pleasure's damaged portrait:
all his handshakes and orations, future

memoirs, vetoes, votes, positions, his legacy,
the traction crackle of a fading painting.

DIPLOMATIC RELATIONS

Lying in the rotting sun, shining white,
the embassy turns its air full-blast. Red
lights blink in the sweep of surveillance

and beneath the stairs, an earpieced mustache
bristles. Clicking jaguar teeth over trade
disputes and tariffs, the embassy mock

charges, chuffs, and pauses for a party.
Plush black Benzes push and wade, hippoing
into the complicated crowd, starched and sutured

with champagne. Exploding corks of advice
spring from the ambassador as he spends
the facts of his frightful life like small change

on strangers. In the square, the park is locked,
the wrought bars a zoo for creepers strangling
themselves to sleep, overgrown and dusty.

With tabloids folded and black suits frizzling,
chauffeurs doze, dreaming of their young daughters'
educations and leather that never

sticks in the heat. A bomb in the Accord,
parked just around the corner, is a glyph
of everyone's grave imagination.

BROKEN COUNTRY SCRAMBLE

The river's applause fades round the ridge
like a candled freedom snuffed by a junta:

wounded echo. Crumbly shale of ocean
plates makes for din of dinner party brawl

while descending in a broken country
scramble from the mountain's shrugging

shoulders. In the kicking crush of footprints,
a micro avalanche of each soul's presence.

Man's a gnawing animal lugging
the ancient crowbar of his want. Woman

too, jimmying, prying her womb open
to deliver a harsh sachet of goods

and bads. Power vacuums all the tiny
valuables into its silk purse of prophets.

When broken countries scramble fast for change
amid the sabotage of mob and fear,

howler monkeys hoot their recognition,
claiming royalty rights to conflict. Ice

slips the sun's gaze each morning while shadow
stays awake. In cracks, a deep kind of wet

leverage, a boiling down through cold, making
mush of that once hard—tough cereal

of boulders sugared with snow—breaking down
rock into gravity's meal, rolling down

to surging rivers. Such broken country
scrambles all signals: order's slipping

into a crevasse, progress went *thataway*,
while the status quo holds tight to sound

bites of dictators and dissolving stones.

INDEPENDENCE DAY:
PLAZA DE ARMAS, CUSCO

The Spanish have dismounted and still stand
at attention on the reviewing stand,
four hundred seventy years after riding
in, their tongues rolling *R's* of refusal

down the throats of Quechua. Campesinos
circle the square, celebrating what? Low
inflation? A fridge in every mudpacked flat?
Rescue workers in gumdrop-orange suits parade

past, firemen in sci-fi mylar hoods glisten,
a battalion of girls wave bloody flags.
The last Inca, Tupac Amaru, was drawn
and quartered here, four horses' nostrils blazing.

Now waxed shoes salute stiffly from jeeps, proud
of vanquishing his self-named children plus
the not-so-Shining Path. Camouflaged boys
roll by, cradling rocket launchers like men

on Moche pots gleefully handling gigantic
cocked erections. Machine guns bloom
from seated crotches. Heroes, mestizos: mutts
all conquerors need, rebar for the concrete

of their confiscation. A seen-it-all dog
in a tatty alpaca sweater snoozes
while mirrored shades command Komatsu
dozers. Their motto: *Moving Heavy Stones*

For Centuries! Bells of the cathedral
clang as flares shoot pink fizzing up only
to come, spent, back to the plaza's tired arms.
On cracked church steps, sweat and urine.

A lone beggar, moon-eyed, blind, picks
his chiming mountain harp in an alley
under the blare of a goosestepping march—
the army band still squawking up the square.

REVOLUTIONARY POLITICS

for Max Levchin

Forced water must be blown, warning lights
observed and blower valves respected

even if a water jacket's compromised,
the spud-and-chain starts grinding, or the stoker's

hole gets monkeyed. Whether towbar toolbox
governor or flywheel piston whistle, any steersman

or oil boy tender knows his crankshaft from his
connecting rod, his sliding valve from his reversing

lever. A rhythmic spiking pressure gauge shows
how every revolution describes a perfect circle.

RATED X

The facts don't lie: women have been chopping
men's members since the first stone tools got sharp
enough. Statistical correlations
exist tween philandering and such chopping.
Take Thailand. The practice is so common
surgeons sport killer re-attachment skills.
So women go to lengths. One took a bus
to a distant province with it in her

purse. Arriving, she buried it. One flash
fried it in her wok while he slept off his
bath of gin, then fed it to the mongrel
dogs of her back alley. In another
famous case, one angry newlywed
tied it tight to a helium balloon
and watched it float away from her Chang Mai
home, north, toward the Golden Triangle.
Touché. Such Bobbitry should no court try.

Darwin's got jurisdiction. Men wore toupees
before women wore lipstick. Women's thighs
are on average two inches thicker than men's—
en garde. *Wedding* comes from a root meaning
to challenge in combat. Husbands are not
pet fish, which, when all looks bleakly cloudy,
may be flushed down memory's toilet or dumped
in a small jar and placed in the freezer,
claiming heaven in a short hour. No.

Pet dogs, maybe. Little lost dogies weaned
too early, range-beaten orphans crying
for mamas to give them a suck, big dogs
in the manger, hot dogs, dog-and-pony
dates who soon face endless dog days in her
doghouse: leftover of the love she used
to have, take him home in a doggy bag.

LEH OVER IN KASHMIR:
ALCHEMY OF TRAVEL

Like a horror movie just before the girl
gets it, or industrial rumble of refining
molten metals, a distorted drone topped
by reedy shrieks keening from a two-bit
speaker broadcasts the local lamas' peculiar

neurosis to a town gorged on tchotchkes
and German bakeries, and contests the muezzin's
cackled barking issued from a higher speaker
(the Allah Turbo 2000) down the same blistered
block. Religion. A dusty rain wipes tans

off tie-dyed tourists and Army Tatas honking
their contemplation of the wheel of life.
Two golden deer, posing as flea-bit drooling
dogs, bark the entire Buddhist scripture
before chasing their tails into the rapid flowing

gutter. You may insert your business
card if you so desire. Check your baggage
at least two hours before all flights
from your job or family. Watch sand spun
into concrete columns behind bamboo scaffolds

and you, wet clay spun by travel into a gleaming
idea of you, full of future, bronzed, absolutely
true—all pockets of stale air vacated, all
prejudices dissolved, horizons expanded and film
exposed—finally ready to return home, the same.

FREEDOM OF / FREEDOM TO

A spiky purple ridge is all that's left
of yesterday. Let's celebrate tomorrow

with all the ease of sheep discussing
dinner: that bit's a wolfless browse, watch for thorns

in the wild rose, don't collies come to drive us
from dessert as if denying us was *theirs*.

Never mind, the hills are blanketed with breakfast.
Some of us will eat it. Some of us won't.

HUSH-HARBOR (THE OLD SOUTH)

In the stony glistening woods, we gathered
after dark, never considering ourselves

slaves then. Wet hay and blankets to muffle
secrets and dampen all the shouting

in our souls. A pot, upside down, to make
noise quiet. A lookout, in case magic

failed. We'd slip free and hide fast
in shining clearing, a moony congress woven

from dim hopes. We'd chant the ocean small
and paddle our way home. We'd pray for snakes

to save us from these ghosty men with guns
and crops. Old rhythms carried spirits, old

rhythms eclipsed facts. Witches and weasels
may have caught us, sold us, shipped us—but they

never owned us. Clotted tongues we'd been given
were now freed, binding hymns were unloosened

into blues. What did we know? What did we
know of hate's austere and lonely offices,

of strangers debating our fates? We made
music. We made trees dance and birds tame. We

made freedom rhyme with misery, cotton
cushioning the flesh of our bright darkness.

BATTLE HYMN OF THE REPUBLIC, 1860–2004

Let us cross over the river and rest
under the shade of the trees. Melisma

of wind carries cannon fire over hills
into the lush valley. Bridges won't last

heavy horses. The river must be swum.
We are in The Wilderness, fighting still.

That side of the tracks is theirs, for now. Gates
close but can be jumped. Accounts stay open

for settling. Metal drift of wind carries
fire of MAC-10s and Uzis over hills

into rich zips. Let's cross over the tracks
and kick back on their beaches with their whores.

PIRATES (*Two Photographs, circa 1875*)

Five men on their knees in the sand, arms lashed
behind their backs. Ships in the calm distance,

bobbing beneath harboring hills. The beach
fringed with natives, some shouldering rifles,

some holding flags. The five kneelers wear white
shirts and loose pants. Squinting, two look away

down their orderly prostrate queue, to see
what's coming. Grub? Swag? Booty? In the next

moment, thirteen unlucky men have lost
their heads: sliced cleanly, mouths slightly open,

eyes hooded in prayer. The heads sit upright,
placed just so on the sand, as if children

had buried their mock-protesting dads up
to their necks for fun between swims. Abridged

versions of the thirteen carefree bodies
chest the beach behind the heads. One head lolls

on the small of its own ex-back, while one
armless native looks on, his innocence

unquestioned. The milling men with guns and flags
have disappeared. Now, nearly taking bows,

eight starched Brits stand jaunty with hats and canes
surveying this production, this chorus

line of crime and song, sword and dance. Tea time
can't be long. Bloody hot. The tide is out.

SPIEL

A young man on a French beach
wading in the light surf and wan sun

backflips into a wave. Nearby, a friend lies
on the sand, gesturing, holding a picnic

of his guts in his lap. In three days, sand-
wiches will be consumed here casually

by those in command, whiskers will be clipped
and cards dealt, but now: only a concrete

pillbox re-upholstering the enemy
with the reversible fabric of his own

stained flesh. For those coming ashore in trembling
waves, a heroic chance to become

a stump. Strafing, sniping, this mortar coil
unwinds. To eat enough fire so those flanking

can flee and kill the pillbox, to lend a hand
or a leg, to have the chest-borne letter home

Swiss-cheesed—the rules of the game.
Afterwards, on the beach, a dead zoo

of young males. Cut to the amputees
being fitted with limbs to blow away

on cue. Cut to crane, slate, chopper,
light meter, honey wagon, bullhorn

and director's chair. Simmer fifty years
or so. Reduce a dimension. Serve cold.

EDGE CITY

Machete elbow of camera slashing pictures
out of context: the local real-estate

photographer. On waffle-slab concrete we chortle
through lunch with plastic sporks and smoking

secretaries. Prick of conscience, Father Flynt
drives by in his leather Cadillac. Parking

valets in mustard turbans throttle Jaguars
in reverse, their breath tickled with curried

heat. The Indian place serves phat amberjack
chapati but a lackadaisical mulligatawny.

The red dots on the server's forehead and keyed map
indicate: *You Are Here*. Boffins of boondocks

with grant funds study the family of lilac-throated
hummingbirds, oddly at home in the corporate

trellis defining the plaza. Entering the software
building, with fuchsia pumps and bag, a soon-to-be

flatbacking hooker carries her box office
with her wherever she goes. Her breasts are

insincere. The ataractic hum of vented steam
cushions sun glare and snarly three-class jets.

A gray-uniformed security guard on his midday
rounds watches the bird-kissing scientists and says

speaking of research he's seen a pack of coydogs
wandering through here at night, eyes shining

in the beam of his flashlight. He spotted them
running down the stopped UP escalator thinking

at first they were stray shepherds. The *beep beep
beep* of a backing Starbucks truck ends his story.

TRANSFORMATIONS

The way lightning touches a deer's antler
on the lusty rock outcrop—foraging

for contact, for embrace, amid the barren
peaks and oceans of the deserted world—

some people use the telephone to shock
their friends with news, to kill them with content:

a bare hug, leaving the receiver stunned,
gurgling blood. So too the swaddled shoppers

charging cross paradisal parking lots,
surmounting barricades, sucked through revolving

doors, reaching out to lance desire's abscess
with a single swipe of plastic or strangled

cash in tightened fist. With faint aroma
of boxed tissue casketing the kills, they're tagged

bagged and tossed in angry chromed trucks whining
under loads. Church bells celebrate the shoppers

home—squirrelly, bulging, packaged, never late
for church. Everything inside something else.

TODAY'S PLANE CRASH

A bluebird in my garden pecking
at the dead butterfly is me.

The shrill *chirp eek chirp* of the dead-
battery smoke detector is

the bluebird. A campaign for Congress
seducing votes is the low growl

of spotted hyenas. Sloppy-troughed pork
products are the campaign.

A flailing standup jokester peck
pecking morals is the Speaker.

The black box tape reeling sticky impact
of quickening terror is the jokester.

WAFFLES

for Adam "Red Dog" Blitz

All the crummy things that happen
on a day-to-day basis—a perfect beer
ruined by the barman's dirty finger-
nails, standard humiliations by unseen
masters on the phone, Suburban
Ubiquity Vehicles jamming our way
from here to there—are not redeemable

like a coupon or bad boy's erection
in Catholic school. Likewise, larger
degradations are hard to remove
from the rug once the stain has set.
Proxy wars, general banditry under
the guise of insurgence, dimestore
massacres, elected anacondas—

a toupee to hide our moral baldness
would dwarf the polar icecaps. Scale
only speaks to the decimal point. Essences,
unchanged by amount, won't boil out of soup
despite our reducing and reducing. All
such miseries—including divorces mixed
into infants' formula, blank-disk kids

jacked on joystick killing games, undone rents
pushing Ritalin or smacking kids or
smacked-out themselves, or gridiron hamstrings
popped—all such efforts need tonic and fizz
to quiet contemplation's turning stomach:
a golden crisp but not yet burned Sunday morning,
dripping with syrup, a trampoline of waffles.

FAILURES

Sometimes failure is just failure and not
injustice. Nothing succeeds like success.

The ormolu of silicone or saline
in a breast presents a strident pageant

smile, but hides in its storeroom a heavy
downshift of anger over the world's grave

condition. The heart becomes a cageling,
trilling *Want Me* in a den of its own

waste. Emetic outsiders achieve judge
status. To each according to his own

firing squad. Most savage crocodiles end
as tiny eggs, meals fit for butterflies

and blacksmith plovers. Most celebrities
got extra extra-rich milk when they were

young, studies show. There they go, emperor
penguins waddling down power corridors

of tube and screen. The way, in war, products
are consumed by violence, your faults get eaten

by those starved for triumph. A ludic bash
on sprinklered lawns, in offices and test

beds, springs march music on the players,
selecting those who stay in step. Elide

from the group photo this one. Let that one
hug herself. Subvert the normal urges.

Sometimes failure is just failure and not
injustice. Nothing recedes like success.

. . . . II . . . Well, You Needn't . . . .

CAPSIZED

in memory of Edward Lewis & Terri Kaplan

Fat Qawwals spin a deep circle of praise
with buttery voices, ticking tablas
and the breathing liquid pulse of silver

harmonium: *Oh breeze Oh breeze please take*
the story of this speck of dust to the sun
up above. A man, swimming among sharks,

a whole fractured night in choking water,
under the shivering bubble of bright stars,
talks himself through it. Around him, beneath

him: three hundred thirty-eight others die.
His wife turns to wax, kissing starfish clinging
to the bottom. His son, gone. When bodies

full of dead air rise to the surface, he grabs two
to use as floats. One under each arm, they buoy
him all night. Come morning, he cuts legs to bits

climbing over coral and crawls onto
a beach, where he's rescued by passing shrimp
fishermen who do not speak his language.

When a cousin dies, at thirty-four, in summer heat,
her baby plunging off the back of her heart
attack bicycle, riding back from the beach, or

another, at thirty-seven, leukemia, following
my father around the endless corner and down
the stairs, we reach for velvet tourniquets.

Try to stanch the flow. Try, can't. But every day
these bodies float us on our oily blood
seas. Every day we wake up or we don't.

HER, FOR INSTANCE

Her body now an overpeppered stew:
so much raunch through the years, leaving flesh

tallowy and slack. The bruised fruit
of her bony thighs and hips, rebar

fingering the too-ripe cantilever
of her breasts. Skin a kind of coarse

deadwood, cells dropping off in a blue fog
of cigarette smoke and backbeat memories.

On this corner, neon liquor and rough
trade coursing the streets in late-model

sedans, saying: *taste this touch*. She stands
with the other restored wrecks, giving it

the old lip lick, eyebrow raise, the old flash
and bend. Such a cult of quotation, groinish

euphuism, embroidering the cul-de-sac sentence
of the day. And this day following the others

with all the vivid piety of ritual and obloquy.
One obstreperous penis after another. A postcard

home to her son. A bottle of Jolt to offload
the taste. Spring blossoms floating above buses

on Bush Street, adding nature's saturnine slap
in the face to the parade of the indented.

THE JUG SHOP

The radio clears its throat of morning
news and traffic as the chardonnays get
dusted. A certain disrespectful grape
is tossed around, then football and girlfriends,
strippers, Osama, growth funds, gin, Iraq,
and finally, football again. Faux sleigh bells
clank at 9:18 when the first shopper
barges in. She needs some help with sparkling
wines. Her price sensitivity is probed.

The woman buys the Veuve Clicquot because
she likes the label. Her brain and body
are gavelled-in soon as she's out the door.
The verdict: too much of one, not enough
of the other. Floods and war, hooded men
the talk show fare at lunch. No robbers come
with masks and guns to suck at money's jugs.
No earthquake makes the bottles fall crashing
to the floor. Bells ring drinkers in. Doors close.

WAITING FOR THE LIGHT:
10:48 SATURDAY NIGHT

He tickles the cactus with small fingers
of water, alone in the fluorescent

store. In the twelve minutes till closing,
he's got filing to do, and math: candy

inventory, late-fee totals, cash count.
I've been in that store. I know the slowhand

way he searches for hard titles and sings
to himself, his gentleness parcelling

the oddball change film rentals always bring.
Who loves him? I wonder, watching from my car,

waiting for my life to change, heading home
with dinner to the same house he lives in.

ANGEL FOOD

The ocean of thought at the bottom
of the barrel, breaking like waves
questioning beaches, is all froth.

The game above our heads broadcasts
everything we're not: fast, agile,
rich. We watch with pleasure, washing

down our losses with this fiction.
The waitress has my mother's name
and is made of angel food cake.

No one mentions politics or love.
The freshly mown lawn of the pool
table reminds me of childhood

Sundays, but smells like spilled bourbon.
A bitter sun intrudes, throwing
shadows onto laps and caps down

on foreheads. This Sunday, we kiss
off everything that counts, drink it
dry, and laugh about the damage.

ALCATRAZ

The tongue of fog that licks my walls
is not a picture postcard. The crooked
street the tourists grope is the heart
of any inmate. Mine is gently bent
into a maze of wrong music and brick.
Water seeps and cracks mortar, seeks
the lowest level, like worms or trailing
candidates. Shaggy clouds slow dance

into oblivion. The warden's nose suffers
Burt Lancaster with a twitch but the plot
fades when he's shipped to The Rock. The cels
of movie fairy tales, the paper gushed
today, had buyers leaping from their chairs:
an animated auction, a forest fire
full of deer, the Beauty topped the Beast,
but priciest of all—the couple waltzing.

Trapped inside a whale or town is nothing
like a girl. Fess up. Call her woman.
And mind or body, call the cage a cage.
I remember loving her, the way prisoners
hate and need their prisons. She's pregnant
now, the word by phone. The baby's doing time
I think and do not say: nine months,
some vague possibility of parole.

WAY BACK IN THE VANGUARD

for Joey Baron

Compulsion. Not a fragrant garden stroll
among enthusiastic peonies.

And the hesitant piano soft-pedals
your prospects for finding a harmony

unhampered by busy signals and trash
cans bulged with yellow paper. An arch of solace

might spring up under heavy battered bricks,
a free ticket for sorrow's lottery.

When lights are low and couples couple deep
in leather banquettes of fractured standards,

press rolls and rim shots, the refrain pays back
the verses for all their grudging work. Who

pays you, pays you back. Stay in back, standing
by the pay phone. Listen quarterless for clues.

Call people you used to know, collect. Call her.
Plead the poverty of an empty bandstand.

VOID WHERE PROHIBITED

This is a frustrating type of song
said Hendrix about "Manic Depression"
while counting blown amp tubes in concert,

About a cat wishing he could make love
to his music instead of the same old
everyday woman. But single you will

dream that daily woman, any fat chance
of a trip to the ladies' room, place
we start and seek all ends. Not surfaces

but hollows, treasury without treasure.
Absence of content and malice. Lovely,
she leaps your sleepless fences while you mime

a chewy advance into her infrastructure:
ball-bearing hips and braced ankled earrings,
vierendeels against the steamed breeze blowing

to the nth power, where n is a man
sitting at the huge drum set of his ego.
Splashy cymbals smell desire gleaming.

You are in the pink when you are in
the pink. Calendars and magazines,
bloomers under swingy pleated skirts

in Cowboy blue, the space configured
for your type but not for you. Abyss
of content and malice, what law refuses

you access? Instead: monthly dose of lad
rag perfection. A little rage builds up
sure. The violin concerto swooning

at the local pub swoons for you, baby.
Any advice Mr. Guy? In polka-dot shirt
and overalls, Buddy kicks his wah-wah

with a grimace and explodes into the bitch
riff he's been sitting on all night amid
scraping Stratocasters. *You haven't had pussy*

since it had you! Street corner putdowns
Dewey-decimaled in every corner of your personal
library. Her lipstick laughs a hollow *O*.

Abscess of content and chalice of bile.
The snow turns bad before it even touches
your head. Virgin slush. Greased metal

rods of rebar in the poured concrete whine
to sour chords. Echoing with rust above
you, the empty stadium of all your wanting.

LOVE LETTERS

Who owns a letter? I've burned them, boxed them,
thrown them in the chopped Hudson. They floated . . .

proving what a lightweight fling
I'd duped myself into. The heart's

thick lumber skinnies itself into shavings
of crumpled crossed-out bleed. Slivers

under fingernails, the sarcastic dump
of mail carriers through your slot, cuts

on your sealing tongue: slow wounds
missives cause, heal, cause again.

Venture off your line, you'll surely deeply
drown. Cast off aspersions, shanghai

drugged promises. Perfumed tyrannies get
pleasured by X, while B coyly pretends

she's all she can be. Truth is always
an evasion executed by fantasy.

DECISIONS

Having a child or having an affair
inverts the equation: what's had, mister,

is you. After test-tube tests prove you're good
to go, possibility winks its skirt

where the rubber meets the road. A buck
fifteen an hour, plastic accepted, converts

fantasy into soul food: *If I dressed
her up myself that's what she'd be wearing.*

What's your e-mail? asks the working girl. *No,
no.* What are you exactly doing? Your

getting-worried wife might call and call
but hotel voicemail distances her voice

on a laid-back microchip. Said wife *made* you: pampered
your ambitions, convinced you your receding

hairline doesn't count, cooked operatic
Italian, but still this scene: flung blouse

draping the lamp, mini-bar plundered, plush
robe swaddling the new babe. Her *Opium*

scent's on your plane ticket home, your future,
your child, this infancy of your desire.

SORRY I MISUNDERSTOOD YOU

The way some people shape themselves for other
people, like water shapes itself for any vessel
or goes to bed with any river, is enough to catapult

Pride into *Too Simple's* toilet. Temperature
too can be conducted through the skin of others,
leaving but a trace of self as scummy surface.

Only the retreat of sleep gifts it back, a lovely alone
zone when you are yourself even if someone else is
on top of you. But sleep's a nightly mold broken

by alarm: upon waking, you must reconfigure elbows
id and superduperego to the glassy fragile outline
of your companion for the daily dance of *handle-with-care*.

A glass-break sensor blinks above every soulless window
of the soul. Butterfly kiss of eyelash, calculus
of seduction. We get broke like every headstrong horse,

sell-outs for feedbag and stable. Seeds leap off trees
in search of children and every son's an extension
of his father's Johnson, out there dicking around,

smelling for some fresh field to plow. Okay, it's all
survival. Is that what you want me to say? I'll say
it: lemmings, elephants, executives, escorts—salmon

wriggling upstream. You can curve yourself into a spoon
for his back or pretzel yourself to his logic, the better
to slide yourself into his genes. Docking maneuver

of the everyday, with whiplash lipstick applied to balm
expectation. Okay okay, you've got other fry to fry.
You'll never miss the water till the well runs dry.

THE GRANDMOTHER POEM

Everyone's got one. How she
holds the family together, makes
special soup (with WASPs it's quilts),
lives deep mysteries and eventually
dies. The death is always beautiful

in bed breathing—*ah ahh*—like so, or
in hospital with the inevitable
tubes, machines and motorized
nurses. Whether it comes suddenly
or takes forever is just fine

print. The point is your grandma
dies and you didn't know her
nearly well enough (but now
that's she's dying or dead you wish
you did.) That's worth a poem

today. Here's mine: She was born
in 1897, mother Russia, natch.
On her first flight she thought
the wings of the plane would flap.
When they didn't, she was so scared

and disappointed she never flew again.
My grandfather (making a rare appearance)
disrespected her for such naiveté all
the doodah day. She had Parkinson's
which made her shake not unlike Elvis

Presley but Nana was beyond comparison
of course. (My grandfather grew breasts
around this time—hormone injections
for a wiener problem—which confused me
unspeakably when I saw him by mistake

undressing.) Anyway, the truth is
I didn't know Nana well enough cause
I was five, she was sick, plus divorces.
My guess is in full flower she was pretty
average. There were candies at the funeral.

SKYLARK

After the Rambler, so mechanical and sideways
on the ice, we thought ourselves lucky
for this new Skylark. Our first power

windows to watch the moon follow us
through trees. Our first bucket seats with Dad
divorced away, his lawyer's suspenders

snapping decreed visits—each Thursday night
at the Pickle Barrel, each Sunday day
at ballgame or howling zoo. Flat tires

didn't scare us. There was gas at every
corner. I wanted the smell of that car
to never fade, and kept the windows closed

against it. I knew another man would
interrupt, dirty the white seats, throw
his junk in our clean and spacious trunk. But

now—my sister, Mom and I, alone together
at the empty movies Christmas Eve, that car
ours, parked, blue, waiting to fool us home.

GUILTY

Queasy feelings my friends will testify
against me, crackling static in the trumpet
of loyalty. Success is a flouncy
nightgown, easily shed or stunk by sweat
to the sticking point. Moral cleavage pains

the victim more than perp's new conscience
pricks the perp. Decolletage shows pendulous
ethics: what a tease, the rich milk of cash
crowing all night long! And my pesky role
in these revues? Out of the red, into

the black: a twirl away from Uncle Karl,
rationalizing the downtrodden, streams
of revenue, cut lilies in blown glass
vases, eating nasturtiums at gourmet
spots while alley'd cats cling to cardboard shrines

in back. The character witness got bored
and went home. The mirror might say a few
polished words on behalf of the plain but
simple truth. Even she's not cracked up
to what she's supposed to be? Melting to sand

as we speak? Turning state's, stool pigeons sing
penny-arcade operettas of indifference.
One: saw my glistening sister in the shower
and did not turn away, greedily kept
looking. Thirteen years. Two: stole my mother's

change from her dresser drawer while she was out
making girls plié to put food in the fridge.
Seven years. Three: wished violent ends to both
piano teacher and nose-picking shrink
by way of commuter-train crossing. Ten years.

I was just a kid but the list goes on
like an old warped record, skipping, skipping
all the way to a special school for those
special kids in nasty orthopedic shoes.

WOMAN TRAPPED BY SCREAMING CHILDREN

Like the Kenyan woman who killed her kids
and ate bits but was only charged
with indigestion (she was deemed
too *disturbed* to be guilty of murder
given evidence of her dim sum

banquet) this supper-class woman so full
of tuition, therapy and chocolate
is being driven stork raving mad
by her kinder but won't admit it
to the higher authorities. Guilt

hisses scratching the scratching
post of Freud: anxiety, adrenaline,
the spinal tap of *drive*. Grin
like a grimace, hug a hollow
buoy, afloat but empty, she dallies

her days lashed to garden-variety
compulsions: pee stains and fevers,
dead fish, done dishes, when to sleep
and to rise, when to button up and when
to zip, and zip zip zip

her wunderkind marionettes, plunging
back through mammaries to the fragile
rigor of her toddlerhood. And when
the gig is up and these kids graduate,
uncertain to return, the tail-chasing

ceremony will begin in earnest.
Say the word *nature* and know there's nothing
you can do. Damselfly, distressed
in her Lexus, airbags on their triggers,
waiting for the invisible collision.

X PACKS A DAY

Every Monday you check into the grand hotel
of your addiction for a meeting in the stingy
basement. The habit that needs extinguishing,
though you think it into raging torrent,
is a jumpable stream of instant pleasure
and pure suck. A slip here or there gets you wet
the way birth does but won't scrape

down to bone. Important failures kissed
too many days and sent you here exhaling
your past by the locomotive lungful. You know
the way history shrugs off whatever happens
to you—irrevocable birthday traumas, bottles
of rye, lies and lines of anesthetic, old fortunes
gambled into dimes, doctors snipping away at Mom—
and the frosted bangs hiding your face are
that shrug. Cut cords. Cut curtains. Expensive

waiting for something better to screw along
turns years blue. What *could be* never is.
What *should be* sneaks out of town wearing
a perfect silver watch and stretches out in first
class, sleep shades on. And you're left raw,
jet washed, in the intolerant microclimate
of your emotions. Again, again, again.

SAN FRANCISCO TO SAN DIEGO

for Steven James

Who mooted the question of place, a home
page for life, the settling on a site where
load-bearing life might stick? Now cul-de-sacs

clone themselves in caustic red-roofed suburbs,
every home corroding behind its wall
of cinders, every school bus burning

with change-of-route desire. Head hunters
know that empty slots will not fill themselves:
lunch, whispers, drinks, kickers, calls, options, perks

provide the necessary romance. House
hunting, job hunting: food around a fire
and fire scorching cave is what we've come to

since the age of Olduvai. More things change
more quickly but stay the same more slowly.
Lucy didn't need broadband to crack

a nut or dig tubers. They'll pay points, coming
and going. They'll eat the brokers' fees. They'll
box you, truck your cars, move your crap, put you

up for days in suites, fly you down for free.
What you leave behind—the nail holes behind
pictures, the porch and fading deck—connects

this time to another that can't be dragged
and dropped: drunk collage of college midnight
movies, green-gray vibe at mom's funeral,

smell and squeal of baby Matt and marriage.
History. Now home is keys and numbers
on a curb, someone's bad taste not yet rubbed

from the walls, a confusing area
code your fingers frustrate. Start again: wave
hello to suntanned strangers, with their beaming

doors and locked smiles rimming your outpost.
Dig through your lawn for weeds. Say hey to whales
beneath your plane, migrating and singing.

INVITATION TO MOVE WEST

I will take you to the rivers
I have known, throw you in and watch
from rocks the current swirl your eyes
in foam and glow, red leaves of hair

dancing in the eddies. Today
north winds butter the cold black glass
of your bankrupt, barking day job
and thin rents prompt paper cuts, but

when you move to this bay the small
globe on my floor will jump, soften,
and drape itself over puddles
for your wagon train of questions.

AN ATMOSPHERE OF ISABEL

If childhood was a plump freckled mess—
your head a bowling ball of grief, lonely
in the library, checked-out from under
the vacant watch of snoring parents—then

these days have the sheen of bright swims
in sky-blue rippling tarns. From there to here
some Houdini act, and how? Every family:
part straitjacket, part oxygen tent.

Standing in the kitchen making abstract
risotto, warm pastry in the icing
of your fancy panties, oblique attack
of Indonesian salmon upstream in

the humming oven, you clean as you go.
The staccato mutter of chopping block
suggests progress. Chicken soups, chocolate chips
the shtetl resumé you've earned. We go

forwards backwards: inside-out equation
yielding ripe atmosphere of Isabel.
From soupy sea to cracking spire, this air
makes engines purr. Turn over, purr some more.

At night, in the windswept Karakoram
of your dreams, you spot a little kinkajou,
a honey bear of jungle out of place
in frosted mountain heights—yet it's become

a balls-out big wall climber, facing
Rakaposhi, knowing all the ropes
and routes, unafraid of weather, its life-
support system ticking in its treasured chest.

MY PROSTHETIC EVEREST

We got the fax by yak: *Weather turning*
worse in three days maybe four—climb fast guys.
Just like last time on that face when my toes

died. They came off, then bigger bits. But climbs
since then have me convinced, and now I love
my calves. A secret edge: steel don't frostbite.

Last night in tent I dreamt of parachutes
and saws, tea time on the summit singing
Miss Otis regrets she is unable

to belay today. Then, an ice cave dirge.
My daughters threw orchids which broke against
the glass lid of my coffin. My wife wailed

and moved to Kansas, where it's flat as death
and Jayhawks sing hello. Now Sherpas bring
biscuits for breakfast and we're back humping

loads. Base camp feels like blackboard fingernails
erasing every angle of ascent.
Humming glaciers plow laggards into chalk.

Mandalas of gravity spin boulders
the size of homes. I wonder if my mail
has found my daughters in their cozy room

with the fuzzed wallpaper clouds. Snow, debates,
plans, routes. We are to wear our sponsor's heart
on our sleeves at all times. Film's paramount

for further finance. Wait for the cameras
at the fourth icefall crevasse (our dragon.)
The narrator's voice will lift the drama

higher tween ads for trucks and insurance.
He'll cheer on risk and wind, while the ping
ping of metal bones on rock adds texture

to the soundtrack. This cold scrape satisfies
all needs of mind and body viewers will
be wrongly told. Breathless, be told

I've forgotten the past, I'm in the moment. Cut.

BELIEF SYSTEMS

The way falling planes at night believe
in their lit runways, the way basketball
players shooting the turnaround believe
in the swishing sound of nets, the way
even the steepest inland cataracts
believe in oceans, I believed in you.

That's not exactly true. There were times
when imaginary earthquakes sent double-decker
highways crashing down on my car, trapping
me for days, legs mangled and pinned under the dash,
the radio stuck, out of reach, playing country
tunes over and over whiny and sad.

There were years when rivers refuted oceans,
when everything I shot went around-and-*out*,
when planes stayed grounded by strikes and metal
fatigue—their swollen empty bellies betrayed.
So to say that planes fly, hoopsters hoist
or rapids froth with full expectation

of deliverance overstates the shaky
crystal case rattling in the temblor.
And the temblor, which we know is coming,
believes nothing, refuses queries, and lives
to break all claims: tarmac, court, drop-per-mile,
me, you, and us—every damn and blessed thing.

COUNTING

for Alan Rath

Sitting up all night, watching the weather
channel, wondering where it will be nice

tomorrow. Humorous refrigerator
magnets cling to their jobs, yucking the scrim

of 4:00 A.M. chocolate raspberry swirl:
plush stomach of secret snacking and fear.

The garbage groaning, brimming, satisfied
with slop, lies under the kitchen counter

and the counter counts to a million each
day for no purpose but counting. Compost

heap, quivering mountain of everything
that happened yesterday, and yesterday

the jester doing the false dance about
tomorrow. Where nice? Where will the frozen

jitterbug moonlight give way to a sprawl
of possibility? Where will the sun

rain down its warm opinions, its toasty
handshake of wink, sleep, and winter wheat?

SWIMMING LESSON

Not quite coked beyond the caring point,
you let a small girl almost drown
then saved her from yourself. Her mother

cried into your eyes the killing grave
you'd spared her. How bad you were then: selling,
using, lying—you'd snort your mother's

maiden name if you could spell it flashing
neon. That swimming lesson saved you too
and now, goose-bumped, salvation squeaks along

with each Grand Canyon'd push of splintered
oars in rusty locks. A dory in fast water.
A desert sun, punishing. Past rattlers,

schist, caverns and falls, you muscle through cold
cauldrons of froth and gorge on huge holes
well-scouted. A clean run starts with a good line.

WORK

They don't like you. They're just using you like
a rental car. They want you to help them. They want
their dominance conveyed on the cellular
level, each day subtly with your coffee, morning
memo and *To Do* list. Christmas cards speak

of friendship, the snowy hug of "God Bless"
salutations, the boss's smiling children
on sleds. You are feeding those smiles, stuffing
their shiny Gore-Tex parkas with the fill
of your labor, keeping those kids blooming

to and from private school. Surplus value
is not a textbook subject but your last idea
starching market share. The gold watch someday
will tick bitter in its secretary gift-wrapped
box. Toasts will ulcerate the spasm

in your bad back, jabbing elbows of nostalgia
finding ribs to ouch. A plate of fancy bow-tie
pasta on your last day, the company treating
of course. They don't like you still. And yet
you liked yourself enough to make work work.

MAN, IN THE MIDDLE OF
THE OCEAN, WITH PIANO

Adrift on a cat's-paw of chords, swizzling
his scotch between every tune, the man plinks
at ivory rescued from a dowager
not sold for scrap but sunk. The Chart Room hums
to the sound of cash registering
above chorus, bulbous noses buying
bluehairs yet another round, the vague snore
of buried engines throbbing out a wake.

Notice here the multikeyed preserver:
how bars of music and money keep him
from his waving kids and wife, how the float
of nowhere clips along like some salt-teared
movie—with him the last-reel loser
everybody loves—and finally how songs
redeem their singers when no one listens
to the words. This one goes out to the one

who got away. This one goes to Audrey
and Max on their anniversary voyage.
This one's for Monk, who wrote charts that keep me
up at night, my fingers bruised and tongue-tied.
The pay is rich and every other drink's
on the house. The cigarettes, duty free.
Still, each noon, he's out in his blue-suede shoes,
swabbing the decks of his expectations.

FOR DAISY, ON HER 13TH BIRTHDAY

A breath, a sigh, a breath, a sigh—you loll
faux savage in the delighted garden,

adrift in dappled maple shade. Roses
and rosemary, camellia and birch, hares

dancing on elephant heads, shady plum
and bobbing apple, star jasmine, kaffir

lily, abutilon, daffodil and freesia,
heavenly bamboo and beryllium rods tinging

in the soft-circling breeze—a zydeco
of impossible blossoms rocks the day

awake. What a dream to wake to from sleep's
deep plunge. Tonight, constant kisses, cake

and a light stroll on the town. Tomorrow,
the doctor. So take in the fickle sun—

suck bliss from each waft of wisteria,
coil and stretch below the pyracantha.

Know each good day's a boondoggle, a birth
day to mark the way you bamboozled

utter nothingness, and out of your parents'
glad panting, made a name for yourself.

PROCLIVITY

for Tony Meier

My wife tells me I'm fluffy. Rivals beg
to differ. The defense rests till fresh dirt

gets tossed by the wimpering few who care
to see my end. Even then, difference

of view clutters airwaves depending on
distance and bent: those who have seen me throw

hats, one subset; chairs, another; running
jumpers, a third. Mom's seen it all. Dad's dead.

In such situations, the wind tries hard
to wipe slates clean for kinder and their creeping

gardens. Culture fuel-injects what nature
offers free: proclivity, the weeping

willow factor: do you like to lie under
the circumstances, gazing up at swirling

branches and their blurry seeds, or do you
prefer staring upright at a painting

of the same tree, buying the kind of truth
family membership brings?—Thursday evenings

free, discounts in the gift shop, calendars
ripping off the days in all their bourgeois

beauty and repose. Monet had his haystacks,
I have my ballgames. Some needles never

get found, some parachutes never open.
I'll see you at my funeral, snickering.

. . . . III . . .Rhythm-A-Ning . . .

LITERARY FICTION

A perfect stranger, he arrived with a suitcase.
But one guest, lounging under the doom palm

near the pool, knew what was *in* that suitcase.
She was a sulky testatrix—her purple

lips a volva of desire—and being that,
she bided her time. She wasn't asking

for trouble . . . she demanded it. Not
the trouble eustasy would cause her ex

shacked up in his beachfront bachelor pad,
but trouble still. She took a banausic

drag of her Lucky, and watched, as the tall
man with the suitcase vermiculated

past her to his balcony room facing
the pool. Room 233. To get that suitcase

from him, she'd have to create the kind
of casual and innocent gallimaufry

at dinner he might suspect. That was her
chance. That was her choice. When the band

started to shout, she'd slip something into his
olla podrida and into something more comfortable

herself. Soon, he'd be having a thrombus
fit for a Southern senator and she'd be picking

through the vomitus for that little suitcase key
that would change her life. She'd have to get

the good stuff quick, throw all the tired bumf
on the firedog, light a match and leave. Oh,

and burn her hot satin black dress, putting on
some old galligaskins to throw the dicks off

the trail. What she didn't know, what she *couldn't*
know, is that the man with the suitcase, now dressing

for dinner in the shadowy light of Room 233,
knew well of her fissiparous plans for his jack,

and vowed he'd never let this Jill get so close
she could hurt him in that way. Never. *Never.*

As the bleeding sun dripped below the horizon
and the poolside band struck up its first koan

of the night—a ballad for no dancers, just the
empty strophes of windblown water splashing—he

took his own measure in the steamy bath mirror:
had redintegration ever felt quite like this

before? Here he was, all his furious smurfing
finished, his long lost facture tight, and now,

at the fag end of the job and perhaps his days
as well, here *she* was . . . again. Yeah, he could

deconstruct the privileging inherent in his gender
role, but how would that unwind his bind? And how

would that trim *her* sails, with him still trapped
in the sweaty genre scene he knew he'd been *born*

for? He shaved, finished dressing. From his window
he could see her, a long-legged kudu with flashing

eyes, standing so peccant, smoking by the deep
end of the pool. He slid his suitcase under the king

bed, told himself she'd be the tutee and he the tutor
on this night, walked downstairs, and dove in smiling.

MILLENNIAL CURVE:
A TORQUED ELLIPSE OR THREE

for Richard Serra

Not dead weight but live load: the hernia
of history ruptures any calm we carry

to the edge of the horizon. Dead calm.
Lacking owls' easy spin, our necks wrench

in backward glance—springs shot from age, cricks
grinding, pocking the periphery. Dead springs.

Is it dawn, noon or crepuscule? Every
flashlight speculates when the power fails

us, and in our urge to round off numbers
we make this deadline slow and sticky: *one*

one-thousand, two one-thousand, ready or
not, here we're from. Such the dutiful spouse

to excitable earth, sued for abuse,
trying to save it like always with sex

or the opposite of sex, a balling
Malthus of action and restraint. Take steps back.

Carry a seascape in your head to sooth
a teething baby. Let lions sleep a hundred

days without a single spoiling fly. Swallow
diamond pills to vanquish *limp* from your gaze,

turn the page on *tragic* with an umbrella
liability policy and a fine-arts

floater. Here's where things get necessary
heavy: torqued Cor-Ten steel collapses

notions of what's hard, soft and true . . . how
rust embroiders our assembly line of days

by stitching hurt to love . . . raw beauty plainly
cooked by cycling sun and rain, salt and cloud.

In morning's middle distance, the tumor
of front-page news begins to shrink and sky

comes clean, all silky and albescent . . .

INDUSTRIAL FACADES

for Bernd and Hilla Becher

Sliding pig iron loading dock doors under arches
A circular window of brick over scraped gates
Fieldstone trim fronting a tiny turntable

Vertical pine planks eaten inside out
Triumvirate of grandfather clock casements
Falling bomb under stepped stonework ziggurat

Leaden turnbuckle anchoring loads
Diamond stones like bordering cufflinks
Silver tube exhausting stink of zinc

Vomitory slots slice infilled sash crescents
Glass brick glazing in mortared grid glowing
Window bars lattice aureole of pane

Ferns sprouting from crumbled cornice
Penile shoot dropping down to dumpster
Spalling limestone whitens crenelated shed

Church of the gutter and bowing downspout
Rail siding door bricked-over and I-beamed
Punched periscope in horizontal triptych

Sodium vapor cyclops attached to groin
Siamese valves prick bulbous pipes
A box locked and marked with a large "F"

Feathery carbuncle of exhaust fan spuming
Ancient family crests pocked with paint
Spinning wheels off spindles lie rusting

Sunburned lips of stucco cracking
And a stairway's landing disappeared
By breathy spray of caustic gunk

A snuffed chimney amid blooming weeds
Seashell scrollwork tickling masonry
Iron-crossed entries sport pimply rivets

Giacometti canisters of chloride stand barely
Speakers jut like church bells in mid-toll
"1900" above the puncturing hyperbolic cables

Eyebrow of drain above vault against rain
Rusting candy cane of spiralled smokestack
A pigeon pauses on wedding cake roof ledge

Veined stack of insulated pipes snaking corners
Spool of telephone wire thimbled on slab
Rosette of ventilation spins against suffocation

Fatigued axles piled like cords of fir
"X" marks the superstructure spot
Birthmark of white brick on the dark countenance

Zigzag clinker staircase in wash of steam
Swiss chalet timbers lodging cinder blocks
Chipped-tooth grin of smashed window

Scratched glass glaring fluttery light
Corrugated aluminum waffling stained snow
Double boilers heeling like leashed sheepdogs

Overhead chevron angling to train entrance
Effluvia tubulet bisecting black skewback
Chamfered corner and steely ellipse intersect

DAYS

in memory of William Stafford

A cool shandy on the sweating screened porch,
the ice tickling air, melting silver chimes.

In the full hug of gulf wind, the weeping
willow curtsies branches, *shushing* the air.

The dog twitches asleep on the rocking
shoofly, sniffing rain in dream, dreaming meat.

The ice splinters the wind-wept willow, which
shadows the dog in the draining sun till—

Tomorrow, and the cool shandy again.

BLANK

for Susan Silton

It's so _____ no one can _____ much without
tiring of the _____. Twister put you in

shapes as a child you could only dream
your main squeeze into as a grounded teen.

Cross words from a boss or authority
figure might make you unspool, feel small, punk

like sick hiding dogs or little Johnny
Rotten. Clues buried in the code of fat

angular acrostics dangle supper,
wet wormy lures to lurking muskie. Air

waffling back and forth in a bass drum tween
backbeats knows not what it wants to be till

the next kick tells it, explaining intent
and thumping it boldly into the world

of analog, sine wave and scribble. Meat
cut from the brisket of your grandmother

might provide a partial answer to this
question of character. Flaming giraffes

suggest another approach. White paint thickly
scumbled and scraped gives up conquered colors

only after intensive interrogation
and light torture: mint, moss, saffron, signal

red, sea foam. Use *blanks* like sun X-rays
empty days. Try the smooth fox terrier.

Now try sassafras. Or: _____ the mother
who would rob choice of all its gravy, boats

their confused and occasional winds, forms
the urge to fill themselves out, then change shape.

S, M, L, XL

for Rem Koolhaas & Richard Eoin Nash

Saraband of anagrams, symbols bow
and curtsy. Stain, take satin by the hand

and wheel her round like a two-stepping two-
timing man. Soon we'll outfit that old Raft

of the Medusa with a disco ball
and a slippery dance floor. Silk and velvet

silhouettes, cold-rolled camisoles, rubber
g-strings: tweaked underwear as outerwear.

How to find an inside without an outside?
Where being trapped is pleasant. Road signs

zoom us smartly towards the efficient
pursuit of the irrational, yet SATAN

still gets spelled SATIN by bright angel-
dusted teens wielding spray cans. Their shiny

self-esteem inflates, bursts, shrivels in locked
black bedrooms. *Aesthetic absolutes prove*

relative under pressure: Cousin Mort
sawing away at a fiddle, trying

to make love to Mozart but paying cash
for a quick blow on the street instead, for

instance. The corrosive hysteria
of such facts flaunts our best wishes. Don't mind

Truth, she's puking in the bathroom, Beauty
retorts in her offhand way, still smoking

despite tooth stains. A thought hurled by cesta
into the future might boomerang

and explode our woozy architecture:
a lava pool of steel and concrete spalling

towards the kind of big mess history teaches
in school. Memorize the dates by test time.

THE ARCHITECTURE OF IMPLOSION

for Luke Ogrydziak & Zoe Prillinger

This appliance is constructed to process
normal household quantities. Qualities

smack another matter, such as: his manners
were surgical, as he white-gloved the house

to within an inch of its pre-stressed life,
pausing to lick then ostrich-feather dust

the closets of all our delusions, replacing memory's
lint with cleanroom futures. "I" is the ghost-

writer behind every "We" spoken—in chambers
sharp or soft, black-robed, teddy'd or buttoned-

down congressional. The statistical treasure
of an election fans hopes and injects desires

with a channel-changing frenzy: a metaphysics
of slack. Each choice a further reduction

in possibilities, each door a jamb and toe-
crunching saddle to step over. The reflexive

souls of women, as seen through the shapes
of their shoes, warp and skid in the rain

of terror bureaucrats impose. When we change
channels or presidents, do we change ourselves?

And given our surroundings—the modern, the good,
The Gap—can we evacuate the projects

before they imprison us? Center as
void. Void as meaning. Meaning as

old-fashioned. The way rhinestones parody
diamonds, businessmen parody prostitutes,

and "Chinatowns" parody cities that used to *be*
China towns: a certain conceptual zebra

bucks across the horizon of the contemporary
grassland, having it both zig-and-zag, black-

and-white, no-fat-strudel, lite-beer ways.
Flexibility is one coping mechanism:

pushed into the sea by semiconductor
fabricators, farmers become fish farmers.

Please direct the bulldozers to the right
locations. All such global, local (glocal)

solutions beg testy questions. A wind
tunnel test may strip all the skin off

your ideas. Theoretical models
are a kind of anesthesia against

the suffering left behind in their sloppy
wake and/or immolating jet wash.

But: the way light glows golden through onyx,
the way light filters coolly through fritting,

or poured concrete's skin shows wood grain
from forms, or zinc reflects thunderheads

and hammers, whispers food to the starving
eye, trapped, surveying the entire plotted

world. Out of clay, out of silicon,
out of blueprint, cardboard and glue, I am

trying to build a 1:1 scale model
of my life on this page. Paper walls

can't keep a roof from crashing down daily,
freely twisting. Rain is not a theory.

MY FAVORITE THINGS

for Nigel Poor

Kisses on noses and whiskers on mittens,
flop ears on spaniels and cops who get bitten,
music that's Dukish providing some swing,

these are, count 'em, five of them. Instructions
include daisy-chain advice to all protesting
closed-fisters: take a small cloth damp with Joy

and apply to the surface in small circles.
Ideologies can quickly be wiped away!
Fancies, mindsets, factoids, even long-held

cherished beliefs follow with the *bing bing bing*
of BBs plucking roadside targets. Move on
people. A finicky liver is either a whiskey'd

war veteran or a depressed pompom girl unable
to face dawn's early light. Drink up: sometimes
the creepiness is exhilarating. Millipedes make

the dank basement what it is. You couldn't live
without them without violating an order
of magnitude. Coalbed sulfur needs your shovel

and the neutron bomb button your finger
like a hamper of puppies teats or a Mazda of bachelors
Ladies' Night at the singles joint. Truth is

Sara Lee was so busy doin' it and doin' it
she hardly had time to bake. It was her *sister*
who had the magic oven, but history

often gets it wrong. Why despair? Banana
cake iced up and tinned remains a steady fave,
despite the cognitive dissonance implied

by saturated fat. Joint ventures geometrically
expand our possibilities. The false plum blooms
and blooms, without fruit or purpose, except mine.

RUSTY CAGE

for Chris Cornell and David Lynch

I'm going to break, I'm going to break my,
going to ride a pack of dogs, rusty dogs,

broken nails, tureen of panther scat
in the heavy bakery, dogs looking for

their bones. Keep the movie rolling keep
the exits chained. She glides out the car

hips on wheels. In the meth compound
the bandito knows the gig is up but won't dispense

with his mask. Sinking quick. Butterflies fly
out his mouth the moment he renounces

violence. Power chords suitable for framing
from a stack of Marshalls. Down on my knees

down on my luck she glides out the car,
second skin, interstitial lingerie. Oil, silk.

The ladies of this land, inferior to none in beauty,
would be the apes of none in dress: a new American

style thrust upon us, confirming red as the new
black she glides. Michael, Scottie, Dennis, Toni,

Phil, gliding. Air, Pip, Worm, Waiter, P.J., dealing.
Old fogey Tex sports a Zennish way: *Run the triangle*

boyz, let the defense name the play. Chain link makes
a mod pattern on her pantherish abs. J.C. and Buddha

playing croquet on a fiery hot day, with Muhammad
officiating sternly from that highchair of his.

Baby goop on linoleum is carpet's gift horse.
Bun Baby & Barbara Bush Pounce On Our Revolving Stage . . .

We've Got The Loosest Slots in Town! Makes the desert
disappear. Against the stinking rusty dogged desert

a herd of roving portfolio managers bay at the poisoned
moon. Tricky time signatures pounce on the unsuspecting

creamy boy, his flannel shirt gaily ripped into a cut-out
of his mother's face. Stop this now stop it or else . . .

Your grandma's toaster will spray flames
singeing her already thinning eyebrows. Another black

boy will get the melanin beaten out of him by the flaxen
pasties of a *good* neighborhood. Those condors into which

we've put so much time and love? They'll fail to re-establish
themselves in native habitat. Indians (real ones) will continue

to mainline gaming profits to the exclusion of sweat
lodge rituals which had always centered them in times

past. Fathers will continue to shove their tongues
down their daughters' throats (those little monkeys!)

only to show up on best-seller lists years later via
their daughters' rusty-tongued pens. Cholesterol will be

darted into the moon-faced butts of fat Floridians
sharing a cigarette with negativity. Board whackings

will rash the pleats off habitual Catholic school girls.
Planes carrying beating hearts in Playmate coolers will

crash short of their transplant targets down in the Everglades.
A panther will probe the tasty spilled meat puppets, the black

box keeping the "official" score. *Chads! Chads! Chads
For Sale!* the official will sing, busking in her ho costume

amid the wreckage televised pretty to a faux rusty Texas
ranch. Out his cage he will glide glide like new damage.

PACKAGE / PACKAGING

A package can change your mind
about what's inside. The way white
takes everything away, drains life

but suggests the possibility of purity,
while black adds life back. The stain
of the black mountain cherry triggers

another way of fabricating kirsch
bottles. These two biscuits equal
one meal, woman making drive-by

purchases need to know. Here the bow
is bigger than the box, each one frilly
different, making every impulse buyer

as unique as the scent of her post-
purchase. Cookies can be people
and batteries cows, giraffes and monkeys

depending on the demographic. Focus
groups don't help much in their bumble
backwards for what they think they like

naturally. What they like is *yesterday*
and what we sell is *tomorrow*, clicks
the marketing maven behind the secret

mirror. A still softer shade of blue
for the softener, and yet a darker shade
of navy for the starch. Now we have it

justjust right for our seducing swaybeat
klepto tango: typeface, color, odor,
sizing, stock, gloss, shrinkwrap, identity.

IF BOOKS WERE LIKE PAINTINGS

for Ed Hirsch & Ed Ruscha

Bidders frothing at their bits to own the texts
would dominate the social pages. Writers would

have openings, chardonnayed patrons backing
away from masterpieces of punctuation, sighing

about the price. Copies would seem such dim
simulacra that all attempts at duplication

would be sneered as marginal, unless simply
by students copying down words to learn style.

Secular scriptoria would spring from venture
capital to satisfy the litho market, but

bourgeois pride in owning such epidermal
postcards void of meaning would be hollow.

Long-awaited novels like *Richter's Candle*
would make auction catalog covers. Well-researched

histories would have the whiff of Tintoretto.
A Pulitzer triples value overnight. A Nobel?

You'd better have bought very very early—before
it was *written*. Owning the ideas would grumble

what's left of the Left, as when The Mapplethorpe
Foundation buys the world supply of Oscar Wildes.

Books would be snatched, the hunts for them daring
and international. Of course security would sprout

its tendrilled apparati, fisheyed and wide-angled,
in pursuit of the purloined. Bookshelves framed

in gold and filigreed, vitrines encrusted with UV-
coated shatterfree plex, low-heat bulbs on remote

dimmers, standard: every book a Gutenberg under lock
and cozy key. Aura would be all-powerful, essential

as a factor in valuation. A busy after-market
in aura would emerge, mature, and be deconstructed

(at a profit) by the experts, who'd not need
to read they'd have read so much. Forgeries

would make the papers. Not A Real Virginia
Woolf, claims the white-coated team of conservators

who had a go at the manuscript. Not True Gore
Vidal Writing Mailer's Fiction All These Years:

X-Ray Spectrography Proves Beyond All Doubt,
squelching rumors planted in *The New York Post*.

There'd be fractional gifts of ideas and promised
loans of concepts. A metaphor might name a wing

of a museum in Texas. Young collectors would settle
for the books of small-press poets. The richest man

would always try to own the wisest book. Insurance
would be awesome, but that's the price you'd pay.

RELEVANCY

None of it matters. Take a look at a contour
map or the flecked and dreamy dark chocolate

of outer space. There is no *wrong* end
of the telescope. Distortion's everything.

Your mom's a sea-chart of all the faulty
sightings your dad made. You might as well

stop reading. But you haven't. Now. Now?
Lurch of watch when time's emergency brake

gets pulled by squirmy teens or living
wills. A warped compass cracking at magnetic

North. South sins and eats its dogs for lunch.
Like I say it don't hardly matter. Neutrinos

parlez-vous and wet kiss strangers. Inside
you, more strangers: HDL, LDL, triglycerides—

motley visitors Hallmark can't target
but doctors drive home in supple leather.

Hammer of space, whacking us into one place
or another. Awl of time, ratcheting, puncturing,

marking notches in the belt tween Big Bang
and this starry evening's walk of hound.

Maybe matter matters not at all. Maybe
the rest—folded outside cells, at large

in the fog, scopeless to the bluest eye—
has a shouting chance if you yell quieter.

DOUBLE BLIND

Ron Saint Germain

Trumpet squeal, rose stink, pepper flame, needle
prick: the eye blinks blind to all, unconcerned

but for color, depth and form. Color is
a cure for language, depth a swimming pool

of buoyant shadow and form a die-cast tool
to announce intention—yet the poor blind

get richer every day. Flourless chocolate
cake. Nusrat Fateh Ali Khan. Lupin

in rain. Furry puppy belly and sniff
of private reserve. Better yet: no judging

the finish in the steeplechase of race,
inflated expectations of wonder-

bra or positioned package, dreck of chrome
and headline. In the invisible kingdom

of sound, music licks sight of its repressive
gaze and ears flower into stargazer

lilies, cumin blossoms, and fleshpots
of sweet and sour. Water, water everywhere.

. . . . Coda

CONFLUENCE CAMP
(*Meeting of the Alsek and the Tatshenshini*)

for Thelonious Blue and Billie Miro

The way wind beats us down then pushes us
forward, the way rivers braid then unbraid
themselves (letting water verb itself
into gravity's rough speech), the way clouds
graze skies in search of each other's thunder—

that's the way we float here, to find sleep
on a slice of blowing sand. Five valleys
disgorge and pinwheel pleasures: lusty pike
and salmon, the pink purple flush of fire-
weed, juniper and alder and cottonwood,
the rivers' bubbling browngray factory
of gravel, eleven hanging glaciers.

Why we come, how we stumble into one
another, how one door presents two more
and two always begs the choice of one—this
is river's song to inner ear: as you choose
your line to run, it has chosen you so

well that physics seems simplistic. Go, flow.
In a constant state of merge, we open
and invade, clench, kiss, shimmy, suck and thrust
into tomorrow, prompting sequestered cells
to jell then split that years later will drop
us in our graves, their tears flowing down
in ones and twos, becoming twos and ones.

SEEING AND BELIEVING

Joel Sternfeld

Rivers fat with spring sliding by
on muddy oiled bearings in dawn blue

Tanker cars of corn syrup shrug
on a siding cloaked by thick brush

Scent of cedar smoke in swampy fog
meanders after the Coltrane rain

The country radio sings *I never been*
a husband but I had a wife I had a wife

Drive-in liquors Save Save Save
Save Gas and sermons' overflowing

Bottled-up church traffic snarling
the multiplex action and adventure

Weeds flower from the tops of rusting
pumps 'neath weathered crossroads canopies

Fighting ivy and kudzu doublewides sprout
satellite dishes asking sky for answers

Bandaged hands pick produce through echoey
buzz of last night's rum and punch

Roadside diners windowed with newsprint
fixing the yellow day the rent stopped

A raven circles in ashes and sparks
above a trailer park trash fire

Four corners of catfish competitive
B-B-Q in the neon bug-zapping twilight

Mockingbird and wren marsh and bramble
creek river rail ferry swamp and swash

Just close your driving eyes and listen
listen to it get dark get dark get dark

VERBATIM: MY AIRPORT TAXI DRIVER, WHILE WAITING FOR A TOW TRUCK, TAKES A STAND ON THE REPUBLICANS

If you don't work, you don't
eat. That's the way I learnt

it. These kids with kids they
just babies themself, you know?

Confiscating the children's not
a bad idea. Give 'em a fresh start

in a kibbutz-type situation. See
Mississippi, we had a long family,

not like today with this nuclear bomb
family, no pop around etcetera.

See we had our pops. But if we
didn't, see we still had family folk

that cared. It wasn't no indentured
servitude. I studied that. But

it wasn't no picnic either. No, no.
We had problem people but not like

projects do. I won't drive there
dispatch or no. We had bad ones—

everybody does. One girl, they stuck
a co-a-cola bottle up her vag-inn-a.

You know what I'm saying? She was
a whore-type. She was a sex tool

of Mississippi. Evil don't pick
a color. Black white pink etcetera.

Most people sit round doing nothin'
watching TV for clues. For what?

Think that box gonna solve something?
I'll tell you what: some concentration

camps are better than others. I want
mine without guns and gangs, TV etcetera.

Say "racism" this, "racism" that. Racism
sure. Anybody know that. It's America,

okay? But after that, what next?